Lowell.

MW01701716

Thank you for your

friendship.

Shorten your learning curve -

and Dare to Get Rich! * !

Larry

DARE TO GET RICH

SHORTEN YOUR LEARNING CURVE

The story of one man's
ruggle and triumph over
oney and the lessons that
ade him a MILLIONAIRE.

LARRY SMITH

FOREWORD BY DONIELLE SMITH

Dare to Get Rich
Shorten Your Learning Curve

Published by Book Ripple Publishing
www.BookRipple.com

ISBN 978-1-943157-94-5

Printed in the United States of America

LoveAndMoneyHacks.com
powered by Success Strategies, Inc.

Love & MoneyHacks

What Others Are Saying

Brilliant! I learned a long time ago that if you want to be financially successful, then you have to study successful people by reading what they read and reading what they write. Larry has laid out his life story, giving us the knowledge to expedite our financial success in this book. It's a MUST READ!

– Michael Dorsey, CEO & President, Dorsey & Associates, Inc.

. . .

This book is fantastic! It's an easy read, simple to follow, and packed with powerful information that can absolutely change or enhance your current financial state ... if you put it into motion.

I was lucky to meet Larry Smith over 20 years ago and have been fortunate to interact with him ever since, both personally and professionally. It's been a blessing to experience firsthand the many nuggets of wisdom that he so graciously shares with everyone in this book. I chose to apply them back then and as a result am in a much better financial position today than I ever would have been had I not taken his knowledge to heart.

These are things we were not taught in school (but should have been!). Unfortunately, most teachers, as smart as they are, don't even know these things themselves. So do yourself a huge favor ... read this book, apply the knowledge, and then share it with everyone you care about. You'll be glad you did!

– Brenda Anderson, Owner, BKA Benefits, LLC

...

Powerful, real, and digestible! I sat down to merely start reading *Dare to Get Rich* ... but read it all before getting up again. It's easy to read and there is no fluff. Larry teaches timeless lessons in a true story form reminiscent of Clason's classic *Richest Man in Babylon*.

After years of learning life-changing financial lessons from Larry Smith, I am thrilled to see them in print so I can reeducate myself and share with all my friends and business partners. This book will increase your net worth if you let it. No pretense. Just down to earth wisdom. It's the financial book the people deserve.

– Harold G. Branch III, Globally recognized author, speaker, trainer & founder of HomeBase Poetry

...

I wish I had read this book when I was 18, 28, or even at 48! It's a quick and easy read. Those who desire to take control of their financial life NEED to read it!

If you are like me, experiential learning connects deeper than plain book learning. Larry shares his most personal life's journey and experiences, for your gain! The opportunity to change your financial circumstance is knocking. Are you going to open the door to the first chapter today?

– Melissa Wilder, Executive Chairwoman, Ladies of Justice

...

I was 32 years old with a small pile of credit card debt, zero in my savings, and nothing set up for my future. I had never taken a financial course in my life. That was before I met Larry Smith. Since then, I have had the great fortune to spend some time with Larry at his beautiful home in Phoenix, Arizona, and that completely changed everything for me. The information in this book is exactly what he broke down and taught me. I had no idea it would be this simple.

It's easy to learn from a guy who went from bankruptcy to millionaire because he relates to where we are and where we want to go. This book is amazing. (I think every high schooler in the world should read this before their senior year.) Thanks, Larry, for the financial coaching. You have changed my family's legacy.

– Michael Fedick, Rapid Funnel

...

If a life well-lived is indeed the true measure of success, then Larry Smith has reached the pinnacle of achievement. Not only has he overcome more adversity than the average person will ever face, he has done so with humility, grace, and good humor.

When you read this book, you will discover how Larry mined important truths from both his failures and his triumphs. You'll learn that it is possible to lift yourself up from even the most challenging situations and to restore your shattered finances, relationships, and dreams. I count Larry Smith as both a client and a dear personal friend. With this book, Larry has given others a peek into the forces that have shaped him as a person, entrepreneur, and investor. Enjoy the read!

– Teresa Kuhn, JD, RFC, CSA, President/CEO Living Wealthy Financial Group

. . .

Dare to Get Rich is real MENTAL FOOD for those truly hungry for wealth! I'm so excited for those who may be where I was when I met my friend, Larry Smith, so many years ago … I was borrowing money from my mom to save my home. Larry taught me to focus on growing my income with practical lessons and philosophies that the world now gets a chance to discover and learn! Larry, thank you for sharing your gift!

– Darnell Self, CEO, Self Defined, Inc. Co-founder, A Fertile Ground

. . .

People say it "takes money to make money," yet Larry Smith proves this myth false. It takes desire, grit, and determination as you will see from his story. In this book, Larry shares his journey so that you can see the path is never clear, but wealth and freedom are somewhere on the other side of whatever tribulations you encounter ... as long as you know what you want and keep moving toward it.

This is no how-to manual. Rather, Larry helps you set your sails so you are pointed in the direction of wealth and freedom, and this is far more important than trying to pin down one specific business vehicle to get you there.

Larry's story will inspire many because we all can relate to the challenges he faced and overcame. To "dare" is to have courage, and this masterpiece transfers his courage into us all. I feel empowered to do so much more.

– Brian Carruthers, 4X best-selling author: *Building an Empire, Money Mindset, Making My First Ten Million, Untrapped*

...

It's been over 20 years that I've known Larry Smith. I am so excited that he is finally sharing with the world what I've had the great fortune to learn in person from him.

This book is not only a shortcut to your financial freedom, it also has stories that the everyday working person can relate to. It will provide hope for people who are struggling financially to truly understand how money works.

Larry helped me identify a much better retirement plan than the one I was on. He opened my eyes to the value of having more than just one stream of income. I know this book can do the same for you.

– Kim Melia, President of Melia Communications,
Co-Founder of Work Play Love Inc 501c3 non profit

...

I have read many self-help books in my life and this is one of my favorites. I have had the good fortune to work with Larry Smith for many years and he is a person who really walks the talk. He has helped thousands of people get started on the right path to financial freedom and this book will help millions of entrepreneurs become successful in their quest for a better life.

This book is a must read for anyone who wants to break out of the daily grind and develop a lifetime of freedom. This book is what I call a "legacy book," a book that will help future generations make the right choices.

– Ross Chantrel, President of Network Resources LLC

. . .

When I first met Larry Smith (more than 20 years ago), I was at a point in my life where a change was mandatory for my personal and financial survival. His story was one that I could not only relate to, but made me feel as if I could actually apply and accomplish what was needed to finally free my family from financial bondage!

I sat down to read just 10 pages of *Dare to Get Rich* ... and when I finally looked up, I was on page 130! Not only was it easy to digest, but rarely does anyone share their actual BLUEPRINT to millionaire status!

Larry has helped me to now become a millionaire seven times over! To this very day, whenever I need financial advice, he's one of the first people I call.

– Mike Humes, President, AFM Ventures Inc.
Mailman to Millionaire, Co-Founder, A Fertile Ground

. . .

Larry Smith has been guiding me as my mentor since 1996. Today, my business generates more income for me in one month than most people make in a year! I'm not bragging, I'm endorsing his mentorship!

Larry believed in me before I believed in myself. He is not only my business mentor but also a close personal friend. He taught me to keep things simple and to always treat my business with the respect it deserves! He has always told me to keep doing what I'm doing and do more of it ... that everything worth value takes time, patience, education, and commitment.

I didn't know anything when I started, but I was willing to listen to Larry. I knew he had the formula for success. This book is a must read and will shorten your learning curve! I wouldn't be where I am today if it weren't for Larry Smith! I'm humble and grateful!

– Christa Aufdemberg, President, Christa Aufdemberg, Inc.

Contents

FOREWORD

By Donielle Smith

What you have in your hands took years to finally pour out of my husband. I can't even put an estimate on how many people have asked him to write a book. I'm so excited to introduce it to you!

Long before I became Larry's wife, he was one of my mentors. I struggled to be successful in my business. I had grit and determination, but it wasn't enough to really thrive. What was missing was an acute understanding of how to make money work for me.

Thankfully, Larry was attracted to my drive and desire to improve; he helped me. He taught me how to properly track revenue producing income, and how to view money as a tool. It made a tremendous difference in my bottom line and in my overall confidence. Mastering money is a powerful skill that will enhance your life in numerous ways.

Larry subscribes to the philosophy that "the master is forever the student." He doesn't do anything half-way. So, not only has he studied money and finances but he has also dedicated himself to our relationship in an uncommon way. He's purposeful in his actions and truly understands the concept of "cherishing."

I am deeply grateful for his continual displays of unconditional love. He's been a diligent practitioner of adoration. I am a fortunate woman! We have so much fun together ... in work, in play, and in our big beautiful blended family.

In many ways, Larry has helped me "grow up" and become the woman I am today. Every day, I wake up thankful. As I write this, I am humbled and in awe of my husband. You see, this book ... it's not just a treasure trove of financial wizardry or a step-by-step guide to understanding the complexities of compounding interest. This is the love of my life baring his soul in written form.

You'll learn about his lowest of lows and you'll marvel at the resilience he exhibited even when life sucker-punched him, so many times. His courage is astounding, it's not easy to retell the saga of your life and to focus specifically on the most challenging and painful parts. But … it's in those moments that his greatest lessons for you were born.

Larry's story will teach you about money. You'll pick up nuggets of information that will be life-changing, no doubt. When you turn the last page, you will have a greater appreciation for the man I am lucky enough to call my husband and partner. You will come to realize that we are all flawed, and at some point, we all chose poorly. You'll learn that it's ok.

My sweet husband turned his poor choices into rocket fuel to charge challenges head-on. Now, he's flipped the script on the past and is sharing everything with you. His greatest desire is to help you change your life.

I am excited for the world to get a glimpse of what an amazing human being Larry is and how much he has to offer us all; as he really has turned his life's tragedies into his destiny. His transparency will move you and hopefully create a desire for you to want to be more and do more!

I am forever grateful for his love, wisdom, and his willingness to always become better.

– Donielle Smith

INTRODUCTION

If we met tomorrow, I doubt you'd ever guess that I struggled financially for the first 44 years of my life. It would be hard for you to imagine me, stressed out at my kitchen table, robbing Peter to pay Paul just to keep everyone fed. The truth is, I was hopelessly uneducated about money. I've written this book to share my life story, help you avoid the mistakes I've made, and to impart some solid advice that I hope will change the way you view and handle money.

In 1995, at the age of 44, I was unemployed, broke, with no cash flow and piles of bills to pay.

If you're broke, or just struggling to make ends meet, I know all too well what that feels like. There are few situations in life that will make you feel as terrible as having no money, especially if you have others depending on you.

Since 1995, my life has changed tremendously.

What changed? How did my future turn from bleak to bright?

In the pages ahead, you'll learn a lot about me. You'll journey through my highs and lows, and you'll begin to understand how a lack of financial knowledge made my life infinitely harder than it had to be.

More than anything, I want to shorten the learning curve for you. I took the long way around! Mastering money will influence your life in ways you won't understand until the concepts in this book become habits. Looking back, I know financial stress played too big a role in my failed relationships, the poor career decisions that I made, and even my health scare. You can avoid these pitfalls.

I found FREEDOM, and so can you.

If your life is improved by what you learn in this book, then all of my mistakes gain a new worth, and we both win. Please take this book and the lessons within to increase your financial education and your bottom line.

Don't take the long way around, shorten your learning curve! I DARE you to get RICH!

If I can do it, I know you can too!

– Larry Smith

FINANCIAL LESSON:

Spencer Tracy said, "There were times my pants were so thin, I could sit on a dime and tell if it was heads or tails!"
So, we can either repeat or
we can evolve!

...

NOTES TO SELF:

ONE

Starting from Scratch

My mother loved a man in uniform.

Three of my Mom's husbands were Air Force pilots. So, I had five "fathers," my biological one and four stepfathers. We were almost always a military family, and we moved, a lot! I wasn't really able to form stable friendships until my stepfather retired when I was 11. We settled in Austin, Texas and shortly after, my mother and stepfather separated. For the first time ever, my mother had to work outside the home. Though she would remarry, she continued to work. My Mom was a very hard worker; she always longed for a grand lifestyle. She dreamed of Cadillac convertibles and a home in the country.

All I ever learned from my mother about money was that we didn't have enough. The phrase "we can't afford it" is blazed in my memory.

As a matter of fact, I never really learned anything about money from anyone in my family. I've never met my biological father, so there was no opportunity to learn from him. My first stepfather adopted me and changed my name to Smith. He was the only father figure who poured into me as a child. From him, I learned to play golf and baseball, how to mow the lawn, how to fix cars, and many other things. He didn't, however, provide any insight into money.

I loved what he taught me, but unfortunately, those lessons came with some pretty severe beatings. Sometimes it was over his lap, but most of the time, it was a firm slap across my head. He was a terrible alcoholic and drank a quart of vodka daily from a brown paper bag.

Unfortunately, physical abuse affects your self-worth. Even today, I still love this man. He spent time with me, and I have good memories. Sadly, he died when I was only 18.

My other stepfathers weren't interested in building relationships with me. In fact, I mostly felt out of place in my own home, like I didn't belong.

If I could have learned about money from anyone in my family, it would have been my grandmother. She actually tried to instill some core ideas, but I wasn't paying attention. I was too busy trying to live the lifestyle my mother dreamed of. In short, I was always blowing what little money I did have.

PAY YOURSELF FIRST!

The only person who ever spoke these words to me was my grandmother. Had I listened earlier in life; this would be a wildly different book. This is, by far, the most important financial lesson to adhere to!

Like most people, I paid my bills first. Then, if there was anything left at the end of the month, I would think of saving it. Of course, I spent all I made. There was never anything left. So, I never saved and I certainly never paid myself first.

Our parent's beliefs and the lessons they teach us influence our future behavior. What are your beliefs regarding money? Where did those beliefs come from? My belief that there was never enough money came from my upbringing and it had ingrained repercussions that took years to reverse.

The life lessons I learned are what I call the Evolution of a Belief System.

#1: Parents, teachers, coaches, clergy, friends, relatives and other people of influence say to the child: "This is FACT!"

#2: The child accepts the elder's perception of what is fact, even if the elder is completely wrong! Because the child does not know the difference between right and wrong.

#3: The child unconsciously ingrains these beliefs in his/her subconscious and builds habits accordingly.

#4: The child grows into an adult operating under dozens of faulty beliefs and habits, though not consciously aware of it.

#5: Then the adult operates under false and limiting beliefs and sets invisible boundaries of his/her life at an unconscious level!

FINANCIAL LESSON:

If you're ever going to get ahead financially so you can build a Financial Freedom account, you *must* pay yourself first! You may think you can't because you're struggling. I will show you *how* you can!

...

NOTES TO SELF:

TWO

Missed Opportunities

My grandmother was an elegant woman. She worked at Neiman Marcus for years and even became Stanley Marcus' right-hand person.

She was the antique buyer and flew all over the world buying antiques for Neiman Marcus. She had a beautiful home in Dallas, Texas.

Nanny tried to talk to us kids about money, but I didn't listen. As a matter of fact, she even opened savings accounts for all of us and put money in the accounts in an effort to encourage us to start saving from a very young age.

Realize the value of money.

Just after I returned from two tours of duty in Vietnam, I had the opportunity to visit with my Nanny. I vaguely remember her trying her best to impart life wisdom to me. On the heels of war, and acclimating to civilian life again, I don't think I could even begin to absorb her advice. My mind was elsewhere.

The lesson to pay myself first and put money away with each paycheck never stuck. Perhaps if I'd spent more time with Nanny, it would have sunk in.

It was another missed opportunity to learn.

The life lesson I learned:

**If it doesn't challenge you,
it won't change you!**

FINANCIAL LESSON:

If you learn to pay yourself first, with at least 10% of your income from your very first paycheck and maintain that consistency over your life, you can become a millionaire! But it's *never* too late to start! I didn't start until age forty-four.

...

NOTES TO SELF:

Three

Leaving Home Early

One night, when I was around 17 years old, I came home late from a date. "Punch," my second step-father, was drunk and angry. My brother and I were 15 minutes late with the car. In keeping with his nickname, he threw me through a sheetrock wall. My older brother took him out in the front yard and beat the crap out of him!

That's when I realized I could no longer live at home. I had to find a better way even if I was still in high school. My brother and I got an apartment together. He loved to party back then and so did I, but when people came over with cases of beer and started punching their fists through the walls in the apartment, I realized I didn't want to be around that either. So, I moved out and found a place of my own.

To make money, I was working at Orange Julius from 6 p.m. until midnight flipping hamburgers and making drinks. By the time I cleaned and closed the store, I'd get home around 1:30 a.m. Then I had to do homework and be at school by 8 a.m.

There were so many bills, I couldn't get it all done! So, I quit school. I left Orange Julius and took a job at a convenience store chain called Minit-Mart, and took on a second part-time job as a lifeguard. My schedule was lifeguard by day, and Minit-Mart by night. In August of 1969, I turned 18.

With my adoptive father, "Smith's" help, I purchased my first car, a 1969 Hurst-Olds. It wasn't just any car. They only made 500 of them in the US. It was a 455 cubic inch with 390 horsepower and all the bells and whistles. I loved muscle cars!

My car payment was $146.11. Funny how I remember numbers so well today because math was my worst subject in school! I failed algebra II twice, and the third time I took it, my grade was a D. I think they passed me because they saw I was trying, not because I actually knew enough to pass the course! The sad part is that I was so embarrassed in high school during this course. Everybody laughed at me, and I felt like a total loser because I couldn't grasp the concept of letters and numbers. The teacher's frustration didn't help either!

Interestingly, since that algebra class, I have never in my life had to use numbers and letters at the same time! Yet, school never once taught me how to balance a checkbook or save money, which would have been far more useful.

Two months after my 18th birthday, I realized I wasn't going anywhere in my life. Working all the time just to pay bills, was no fun. I was immature and didn't bring much value to anybody else, so a meaningful relationship was out of the question.

My stepfather, Smith, was a highly decorated Air Force pilot from World War II. I would have loved to follow his path, but without a high school diploma, there was no way I could join the Air Force. So, I joined the Army instead.

Immediately, I was faced with a problem. My base monthly pay in Basic Training was $87.50 but my car payment was $146.11. My car (the only thing I felt had any value in my life) was going to be repossessed by the bank!

Thankfully, the JAG office had an answer that worked. There was a bill called the *Soldiers and Sailors Civil Relief Act of 1940* which saved my car for me.

The life lesson I learned:

Everything in life you are going through is preparing you for what you've asked for!

FINANCIAL LESSON:

There's never a *debt* problem, there's only an *income* problem! Focus your energy on making more money and getting out of debt.

...

NOTES TO SELF:

FOUR

Vietnam and Back

About a year earlier, a couple of my high school friends joined the Army. After Basic Training, AIT, and Jump School, they volunteered for Vietnam, so I did the same.

One unexpected thing I learned was that the money we earned in Vietnam was tax-free, even though I didn't truly understand the real value of that at the time. I was able to draw combat pay and jump pay, which added to my paycheck.

By May of 1970, at 18 years old, only seven months after I enlisted, I was on my way to

Vietnam. I volunteered for a second tour before my first tour had even ended.

About four months into my second tour, my unit was sent back to the US due to cut-backs. I was out of the Army six months early and I was thrilled!

Looking back, I have good and bad memories from my days in Vietnam. I was decorated with the Bronze Star Medal, four Army Commendation Medals, among others. Our unit received the Vietnam Cross of Gallantry and two Presidential Unit Citations.

In spite of all of the military decorations, when prospective employers found out I had been in Vietnam, they wouldn't hire me! My very short resume with a gap of three years was a dead giveaway.

Time after time, I was told, "We have no openings right now, but we will keep your resume on file." It didn't take long to realize that it wasn't even the gap in my resume that was the problem, it was Vietnam. The stigma of the war was pervasive and the discrimination my fellow veterans and I experienced afterward was incredibly disheartening.

The Army was willing to pay me $300 a month, tax-free, unemployment for 12 months after I got back from Vietnam, but I didn't want assistance. I wanted to work and earn my own income.

Eventually, I landed a job.

The life lesson I learned:

The best way to guarantee a loss is to give up and quit! You are not in competition with anyone else! Live your best life now. Just plan to outdo your past, not other people!

FINANCIAL LESSON:
You can't have million-dollar dreams with minimum-wage work ethic!

...

NOTES TO SELF:

FIVE

Landing a Job

The job? I was finally hired by Kroger as a stocker on the graveyard shift. The pay was less money than I would have received from unemployment. I just didn't want to be paid for doing nothing. I wanted to build something!

Working for less money than the Army's unemployment was good for my work ethic and work discipline, but I was living paycheck to paycheck. After a few months, I added a part-time job at the Minit-Mart, where I worked while in high school. When an opening for an assistant manager at the convenience store came up, I applied for it, and got it!

Working at the convenience store six days a week was pretty fun. It was an era where mothers would pick up their kids after school (often in Mustang convertibles!) and swing by to get a gallon of milk and a loaf of bread. They would leave their purse on the console, pull out their wallet, and leave the car running with the top down.

Can you even imagine doing that today? It was safe back then, and people were still courteous! I would always carry their groceries out to their car, open the front door for them, and put their groceries in the backseat. My adoptive father, Smith, taught me excellent manners.

I loved working there. I grew up in the neighborhood and my customer base was growing!

Before too long, the owner of the convenience store chain gave me the opportunity to franchise the store. My earnings would be 10% of all grocery sales from the store and $0.01 per gallon of gas that was sold. This was back when gasoline prices were 19.9 cents per gallon!

I took him up on the franchise opportunity and ended up making about $700/week or $2800/month. Checks that bounced or inventory shortages were also my responsibility, but it was never a problem.

The money was rolling, or so I thought. I was making more money than a lot of people were back then, and because of the franchise opportunity, I was subconsciously developing a business mindset.

Though managing that store was easy for me, I still had no financial education. My logic was pretty simple:

> ***A) Make money***
> ***B) Spend it***
> ***C) Have fun***

Remember, I still wanted (like my mom) to live the lifestyle of the rich and famous. So, I bought a Corvette!

I looked for ways to increase sales in gasoline and groceries. I got creative and developed business growth strategies. It took about 18 months before my efforts got the attention of the owner. I think he felt like I was earning too much money.

Interestingly, the store chain offered me a supervisory position with a company car, if I would move to Houston, Texas and manage five stores. I would visit each one every day and check up on all the details.

It meant less money, but I was thrilled to have a title. To me, that meant I was becoming somebody, based on my flawed understanding of what it meant to be successful.

This was the 70s, and unbeknownst to the USA, we as a nation were about to experience massive gasoline shortages. If you remember, the shortage meant gasoline allocation, which required you to only get gas every other day based on the last number of your license plate.

You couldn't just go get gas anytime you wanted. And if you happened to miss your day, you still had to wait until your allocation day.

As the gas shortage got worse, people filled up their cars and extra gas cans. Gas started running out. We even had trouble keeping our stations fueled up because the fuel company supplying us was running out of fuel as well.

All five stores closed, and I was out of a job.

The life lesson I learned:

You can't control what other people do, you can only control what you do!

FINANCIAL LESSON:

When an employer releases you from employment, they stop paying you! When you work for someone else, you have no control about your financial future. There is no way you were born to just pay bills and die!

...

NOTES TO SELF:

SIX

My Own Business

With my big "title job" in Houston gone, I moved back to Austin and immediately went to work at the same convenience store in my old neighborhood.

Amazingly, my mother had inherited a significant sum of money from the passing of a couple of her former husbands. She offered all of her children (we were grown adults by this time) the opportunity to start our own business, and she would finance it. Payment would be the same interest rate that her CDs at the bank were paying her.

"Work like there's someone working 24 hours per day to take it all away from you."
– Mark Cuban

No one in the family took her up on her offer, except me. I opened Larry's Liquors, with her help, right across the street from the convenience store I had been working at. I knew everybody in the area and the business was an overnight success!

In fact, we had to double the size of the store within four months of opening to handle the growth. Business was great and we were having fun running the business together.

My mother always used to threaten us children, by saying that if she didn't like what we were doing that she would "take us out" of her will.

Turns out, she was serious!

The store had been open about 18 months when one day Mom told me she'd "take me out of the will" if I didn't break it off with the girl I was dating.

I didn't believe her and I didn't break things off. To my surprise, that's exactly what happened. When I came to work a few days later, my keys wouldn't work on any of the doors; all the locks had been changed! When I went to the bank, I discovered that my name had been taken off the bank account. I was no longer co-owner of Larry's Liquors!

This naturally created a lot of tension within the family. I made her remove my name off the business and come up with a new one. Instead, she decided to buy a building across the street from where the store was and sell antiques, books, and booze.

She was well-connected in the community too, and her business quickly surpassed the success of Larry's Liquors.

The life lesson I learned:

Zig Ziglar said, "What comes out of your mouth is determined by what goes into your mind!" I was still way too immature to allow me to "waste" my time on personal development!

Financial Lesson:

Money isn't everything, but being broke isn't all it's cracked up to be either!

...

Notes to Self:

SEVEN

Joining the Big League

Once again, I found myself without income, so I went looking for a job. I answered an ad in the *Austin American-Statesman* for an entry-level job with the Pillsbury Company.

The job required a college degree. I only had a GED. I used my military decorations as my "education" on my resume.

Without a college degree, I was sure my great resume would be thrown out. Incredibly, they called and scheduled me for an interview!

When I walked into the Holiday Inn where the interviews were being held, I was alarmed to see that all of the other prospects had on much nicer suits than my own.

One after another, those candidates were interviewed. Soon, the room was empty and I was sitting in the lobby by myself. I went to the room where they were interviewing and told them I was called for an interview but hadn't been invited to the room yet. They looked at their list. I wasn't even scheduled. Since I was there, they invited me in for the interview.

I interviewed with the district manager for Pillsbury and it went well. He invited me for a second interview with the regional manager in the next room.

While we were talking, I boldly stated, "Gentlemen, I grew up here and I know everybody. It will be the biggest mistake ever if you don't give me this opportunity, for both you and me." I had no idea where those words came from, but they did come out of my mouth!

They thanked me for my time and said they would call me back. Two days later the phone rang. They were very impressed with my interview, but because the company required a college degree and I only had a GED, I would need to take some tests.

Due to boredom, I wasn't a good student in school. Testing was not my strong point! Despite my struggles, I scored well on the Pillsbury tests and they hired me!

The life lesson I learned:

Don't let someone who gave up on their dreams talk you out of going after yours!

FINANCIAL LESSON:

It's better to fight for something than to live for nothing! If you want to make your dreams come true, the first thing you have to do is wake up.

...

NOTES TO SELF:

EIGHT

Stresses of Life

A lot happened during my first year with Pillsbury; I got married and our first child was born. Shortly after, I was transferred to San Antonio. I wanted to be a responsible husband and father so we found a home.

The payment was $267 monthly on our brand-new, three-bedroom, two-bath house. I had no earthly clue how I was going to pay for it! Even with my newest raise, my monthly income was only $744 per month. Thank goodness for the "One Dollar Down" VA loans from my GI Bill. Still, I had to sell my Corvette to qualify for the loan.

All the new expenses were more than I was prepared for. Some people lived paycheck to paycheck. Well, I was living between checks! I was writing checks without money in the bank, hoping that I would be paid by the time they cashed the check.

Our expenses grew! Then, one day I learned about the "magical thing" called a credit card!

My financial education was virtually zero, so I saw this as a whole new income stream. What's not to love about only paying a small amount each month and being able to buy whatever I needed or wanted?

What I didn't realize was the obvious: that interest compounds over time. My debt load increased; since I paid the minimum amount each month, I was able to get more credit cards with even higher lines of credit.

If you learn from defeat, you haven't really lost.

In addition to living paycheck to paycheck, I now had a huge amount of credit card debt to pay off. I was easily spending 125% of my income each month.

Living way beyond our actual income brought intense financial stress, but we had no idea how to get out of our predicament. After all, I had a good job with a salary, company car, and an expense account.

I still had NO financial knowledge, whatsoever.

To me, "financial freedom" meant I could pay my bills and also be seen by my friends as "successful."

Truth be told, I wasn't financially free at all!

The life lesson I learned:

It's not what happens to us in life that matters! It's how we react to what happens to us that's important!

FINANCIAL LESSON:

I used to care what other people thought about me until I tried to pay my bills with their opinions!

...

NOTES TO SELF:

NINE

Wanting More

Not long after we were settled in San Antonio, Revlon offered me a job several hundred miles away in Louisiana. The offer came with a lot more money, and I planned to take it!

My regional manager from Pillsbury flew in. He rented a car and drove me out to the country to talk. He was adamant about how bright my future was and that a better-paying-job might not necessarily be the best way. All I could see was the stress relief I thought more money would bring.

Once again, I missed the opportunity to listen to someone else's wisdom!

My financial stress was unbearable. A job that paid more had to be the answer. I simply had to make more money to get out from under the debt load.

I accepted the job with Revlon and moved to Lake Charles, Louisiana. Our second child had just arrived. Sadly, I only lasted about four months with Revlon. It was just not a good fit for who I was and who they wanted me to be.

Our house in San Antonio had not sold, so we moved back in. Once again, I was unemployed, and the bills, well, they just kept coming!

You would think I would have learned something or **anything**, by that point!

Fortunately, a good childhood friend had a construction company and he hired me to help dig post holes so I could earn a little income.

I'm convinced he didn't really need my help; I think he felt sorry for me. Either way, I really needed the work and appreciated the opportunity. How fortunate I was to have this good man in my life!

Many have said it, and it's 100% true ... the only place you will ever see SUCCESS before WORK is in a dictionary.

It took some humility, but I called my former regional manager at Pillsbury and told him I had left Revlon. He, in turn, made some phone calls and was able to offer me a job, but it would mean moving to Houston. I took it!

We found an investor who gave us $3,500 to assume the loan on our San Antonio home so we could get some cash to relocate. We loaded up a U-Haul truck and moved to Houston. It felt great to be back with the Pillsbury company. I really enjoyed working for them.

Not long after, I got a raise and my wife landed a job. For the first time in our marriage, we found ourselves with extra money!

Guess what we did with it? Yes, we learned how to live on every penny of it, and then some!

It wasn't very long before we were in trouble, again.

The life lesson I learned:

Einstein once defined insanity as doing the same things over and over and expecting different results. So incredibly true!

FINANCIAL LESSON:

Your mistakes do not define you … they give you the opportunity to reinvent yourself and find your financial success!

…

NOTES TO SELF:

Ten

Sudden End

In Houston, we rented an apartment. We really missed being homeowners and having room for our kids to play. We found a house and were able to get a really good deal with the builder. We qualified for the loan, our new mortgage payment would be $467, which was a lot more than I could imagine or really afford!

I did realize that it was high, but I justified it with the tax deductions I would get from interest and taxes and also how much my net mortgage payment would be, plus the equity growth I would receive. Then, I worked long hours trying to impress my boss so I could get another raise.

Financial success is more about logic than justification.

One night, while working late at the Pillsbury regional office, I received a call from my younger stepbrother. He informed me that my mother and stepfather had been shot at their liquor store.

I immediately called my regional manager to ask for help in completing the task I was working on. I'll never forget his kindness during this time. He even picked me up in his van at 10:30 p.m. that night, drove downtown to pick up my sister from her home, and then drove us both to Austin to my mother's home.

My mother passed away immediately, and by the time we arrived in Austin, my 4th stepfather had also died.

I needed some time to sort things out. I didn't want this catastrophic event to define me. I spent the week in conversation with God. Instinctively, I knew something so heinous could impact me in a life-changing way and I took the time to try to sort it out the only way I knew how ... in prayer. I returned to Houston, ready to face the world.

The life lesson I learned:

If you don't heal what hurts you, you'll bleed on people who didn't cut you!

FINANCIAL LESSON:

Get financially educated! Read ten pages of a good book every day. That's 300 pages per month, or about ten to twelve books per year. In five years, you won't even resemble the person you are today.

...

NOTES TO SELF:

ELEVEN

Unexpected Costs

As I turned to face the world, my marriage ended in divorce! My wife and I always fought about the lack of money, but some people still blame it on my mother's death. I'm not proud of this part of my life; I wanted to be married for life! We made enough on the sale of our home in Houston to pay off all of our debt.

Unfortunately, money remains a top cause of divorce.

My lack of financial knowledge would cost me far more than I had ever expected.

The life lesson I learned:

Unfortunately, first marriage divorces are way too high, anywhere from 40% to 50%. Sadly, a common thread for the majority of divorces includes money problems. In fact, a lot of studies suggest that money problems in a marriage are the #1 cause of divorce. The main reasons are poor communication, no savings, money secrets, and different money values.

Financial Lesson:

It's critical that married couples communicate monthly about finances to ensure they both stay on the same track, even if only one of them handles the money. You should have financial goals to help you achieve your financial dreams together and ensure paying "you" is the *first priority* every month!

...

Notes to Self:

TWELVE

Climbing the Ladder

Six months after my divorce, Pillsbury offered me a district manager position in Denver, Colorado. I took the job and bought a condo nearby.

Meanwhile, my children remained in Texas. I refused to be an absentee father, so once a month I flew from Denver to Austin and spent the weekend with my children. Today, I realize that was 3 days out of 30, or only 10%. I was so unwise and immature at that point in my life!

The round-trip airfare, hotels, meals, rental cars, and entertainment added up. My credit card debt started mounting again. I thought being a responsible father was more important. My idea of what a responsible father looked like was very misguided.

Within 12 months, I was offered a corporate position in Minneapolis, Minnesota. I had been in Minnesota before when the wind chill factor was 60 degrees below zero. I knew I could not live under those conditions for two years, which is what the job would have required, so I turned down the offer.

Soon after, a Pillsbury friend became vice president of a big company in Dallas, Texas and offered me the position as director of sales at that company.

It would mean a pay increase, which was good. I also knew that turning down the Minnesota job offer was a strike against my future at Pillsbury; I knew they wouldn't keep me long-term.

Dallas was only 200 miles from my children, which meant I could see them every other weekend, as the court awarded me, instead of once a month, so I gladly accepted the job and moved again.

Every two weeks, I would drive 200 miles and pick up my kids and drive 200 miles back to Dallas so we could have a day and a half together at their second home, instead of a hotel. I did that for five years, from 1983-1988.

In 1985, I remarried. We had two beautiful children together and she had another beautiful child from her first marriage. Then, in 1988, the company I was working with changed directions and asked me to take a different position for less money.

Allow time to work for you. Remember FEAR simply means you don't have enough education or information on the subject. If you are afraid of something, study and surround yourself with mentors.

In other words, I was given two choices: be demoted or quit. So, I quit. Once again, I was unemployed with no cash flow, but those ever-present bills, they kept coming.

The life lesson I learned:

It's not what happens in life that really matters, but how we react to what happens in life!

FINANCIAL LESSON:

As Steve Siebold says in his book, *How Rich People Think*, the "middle class worries about running out of money, but world class thinks about how to make more money!"

...

NOTES TO SELF:

Thirteen

Launching Out

With nowhere to turn, I decided to cash in my 401K and start a little construction company. I was good with my hands, so I figured I could make it work. I called it Dynamic Designs with a logo that said, "Our only job is making you look good."

While I was focused on making other people and their homes look good, it didn't look very good for me when I had to pay the penalties and taxes for cashing in the 401K. I would not recommend anyone do this!

I built privacy fences (with galvanized posts so they would last longer) as well as sheds in people's backyards. I purchased a Chevy Silverado and outfitted it with all the tools necessary to work my business. Then I hired my first employee.

We did quality work and it paid our bills, but after a year and a half, I knew it would not be enough to sustain what I was going to need to be a good father.

So, I closed the company down.

Why didn't I sell it? That's a good question!

The life lesson I learned:

You can either work for someone else and build their dreams, or you can build your own. The only dreams that have the possibility of coming true, are the ones you actually dream!

FINANCIAL LESSON:

As Robert Kiyosaki says, the S quadrant in Cash Flow Quadrants, stands for Self-Employed, which means you own a job! (That's why I didn't think about selling my company. Even though I owned it, I felt like it owned me.)

...

NOTES TO SELF:

Fourteen

Going Bankrupt

Establishing my construction company with all the materials and tools I needed created another mountain of debt. With no cash flow, I was again in trouble.

You would think that at some point I would have learned something ... anything! I just knew that I had to push through and keep going.

The financial stress continued to grow. I didn't want to stay in Dallas. I interviewed for a job back in Denver where there was an opening with a food broker. I was offered the job with a start time in two weeks, so we loaded a U-Haul truck again, towing my Chevy Silverado, and off we went from Dallas to Denver.

Don't believe negative thoughts about money.

If you ever watched the *Beverly Hillbillies* TV show, that's about what we looked like.

We checked in to our hotel only to receive a phone call two days later explaining that the food broker had lost their biggest supplier and that my job offer had been withdrawn!

This was devastating! Once again, I was unemployed. I only had about $3500 to my name. By some miracle, I was able to purchase a home on a land contract. I got a newspaper route, throwing papers at 3:30 a.m., just to put food on the table.

In less than a year (it was 1989), I could no longer sustain the debt and I filed for chapter 7 bankruptcy.

Filing bankruptcy was the most humbling experience of my life. I fought hard to avoid it, but nothing was working out.

The life lesson I learned:

Pain is inevitable, but suffering is optional!

FINANCIAL LESSON:

If hard times make you do one thing – *never return to them* – then it was worth it!

...

NOTES TO SELF:

FIFTEEN

Health Scare

In the chaos of bankruptcy, I was not a present father. I was physically there, but I was mentally elsewhere. I attended my children's soccer, baseball, and football games, but my mind was always preoccupied with a lack of money. I was haunted by my mother's words, "you'll never turn out to be anything."

Looking back, this still breaks my heart. I cannot regain the time I lost with my children. It's gone. I worked hard to support my children, and I paid my child support on time. I didn't give them the time I feel they deserved because I was too busy trying to provide for them.

It's uncomfortable to share this, it's uncomfortable to remember this time. It was so important to me to be a great Dad. I grew up having five different fathers and had a lot of unpleasant memories from those experiences. I wanted my children to have happy childhood memories. My childhood was filled with conflicts that I never knew how to solve, and that theme carried into my adulthood. No excuses, just reality.

It took a year, but I was finally able to land a good job with a bakery wholesaler. Denver was a brand-new branch for this company. Due to my previous relationship with Pillsbury in Denver, I was able to help the company grow very rapidly in a pretty short period of time.

In fact, we grew so quickly, the company had to move to a new location with a much bigger warehouse.

My schedule was crazy. I would go to the bakeries at 2:30 or 3:00 a.m. and work until 5:00 or 6:00 p.m. Then I would go home and do paperwork and reports. I had no life except work and sleep.

In early 1991, at the age of 40, I found myself in the emergency room experiencing what I thought was a heart attack! Fortunately, my heart was fine. The doctor informed me that the stress I was under would and could absolutely kill me. That was my first wake-up call that something had to change!

I slowed down a little. When my grandmother passed away later that year, I asked my boss if I could take a week off and go to her funeral. He agreed.

When I returned, the vice president of the company asked me to meet him for coffee at a local restaurant. My gut was telling me that something was up. It didn't feel right. Sure enough, they fired me and replaced me with the CEO's 25-year-old son.

How many times have you had money come to you that you

wish you would have invested or stored?

The son had absolutely no experience, but they didn't care. Thankfully, they gave me a severance package, but, once again, I was unemployed.

Someone else was making my career decisions for me! I didn't own the company, so I had no say in the big decisions.

On the upside, the passing of my grandmother unexpectedly brought me an inheritance of $78,000. But with no financial education, how long would it last?

The life lesson I learned:

Proverbs 13:11 says, "Wealth (not earned but) won in haste or unjustly or detrimental use (such riches) will dwindle away, but he who gathers little by little will increase (his riches)."

FINANCIAL LESSON:

Just having money does not mean you "have money!" You need to find a way to turn money into more money! Never give up on what you really want to do! The person with big dreams is more powerful than the one with all the facts! Get fired up with enthusiasm and people will come from miles around to watch you burn!

...

NOTES TO SELF:

Sixteen

Family Business

Soon after I received my inheritance, my wife's brother showed up at our house with the idea of building a new business in Hot Springs, Arkansas. He was so talented he'd been featured on CNN.

My wife and I discussed it. We relocated to Hot Springs and provided the financing in exchange for a portion of the business. It made good financial sense because we thought it would be a hit.

I still had zero financial education!

We found a location for a storefront. It took three months to gut the building and prepare it to be what we were calling, "The Glass Castle."

Just as everything was almost finished, my wife and her brother got into a severe argument. Tempers raged and he became violent and choked her. I was at our house when she drove up in our van with a U-Haul trailer attached. She was terribly upset and crying. She informed me that she was moving back to her hometown in Omaha, Nebraska. It didn't take her long to grab the few things she wanted, plus our three children, and off she went by herself.

When my wife left, her brother wanted to renegotiate the contract. He said we were asking for too much of the business and that he would not open the business unless we changed it.

Let this be a lesson to always seek legal counsel before entering into business with anyone (especially family). The business was not successful.

I soon moved to Omaha to be with my wife and children. Thankfully, the person we purchased our house from was kind enough to give me the $10,000 down payment back. Yes, that money came from my inheritance. I have no idea why the owner gave us our money back, except that God must have been watching over me again.

In Omaha, I was able to get a job selling shoes at a department store chain, thanks to my brother who was a manager for that chain in another city. At least I had a paycheck coming in, albeit a small one.

It was at this point that I was first introduced to network marketing. (Note: I am not saying you should get in Network Marketing, but I made the decision to do so.)

A friend called me and told me about a company that offered leveraged income. The whole concept sounded fantastic to me. It wasn't making money off of other people by taking what was theirs. Rather, by helping them build their business, the company would pay me additional compensation or a commission, and that money was residual!

Don't just spend money, be patient, and allow time to work for you. Time will pass anyway, so use it to your advantage.

The company was located back in Denver, so I made a road trip to meet the owner and find out more about this business. Because of all my contacts in Denver, I was promoted to a higher commission level within 24 hours of entering the business. I thought I had found the dream I had been searching for!

I went back to Omaha and opened a small office space across the street from the house we were renting. I went to work very aggressively telling others about these amazing products and how offering them to others could help enhance their financial goals in life.

It wasn't long before I was the top distributor in the company! The problem was that I was only making about $750 a month. Even with my quarterly bonus based on the company's total volume, my average income was only about $2500 per month.

The company's compensation plan required me to have a certain amount of personal volume and group volume each month in order to get my check. Because I could not maintain the higher volumes, I ended up buying the product from myself to keep my sales up, which reduced my net income to about $1700 per month. That was not too bad, but it certainly wasn't enough income.

After more than a year of this, I called the owner and told him I could no longer stand in front of people at events and tell them they could change their lives by being a part of his company. I explained that if I was the top money earner and I was struggling financially, how could I possibly stand in front of the room and tell people they could change their lives?

I felt like a fraud. My integrity would not allow me to deceive people, no matter how much money I was being paid.

After our conversation, he terminated me and began telling all my closest friends (whom I had recruited into his company) that if they contacted me, they too would be terminated. The lies he spread about me hurt incredibly, yet I couldn't tell the truth to my friends or I would jeopardize their income. It was one of the most painful experiences of my life.

While this was a sad outcome for me, it was even sadder for the owner. About 10 years later, a friend shared a news story with me that the owner was murdered and found in a ditch north of Denver.

The life lesson I learned:

The only people mad at you for speaking the truth are those living a lie! Keep speaking your truth!

FINANCIAL LESSON:

Most people don't have the patience to build a part time business for three years in order to develop a NEW PASSIVE INCOME STREAM that can pay them without having to work. Yet they have the patience to go to work for 40 or 50 years, but when they stop working the company stops paying them! Everything is based on how we THINK!

...

NOTES TO SELF:

SEVENTEEN

In the Bag

After the termination, I was back on the job hunt! I found an opportunity with a company as an independent contractor selling advertising on pharmacy bags. In my first week, I made $1000!

I invited a friend to sell advertising with me. He joined the company and we were doing pretty well … until we found out three months later that the owner of the advertising company was pocketing all the money!

He was not printing the pharmacy bags, as promised. All the paid advertising revenue was going in his pocket! Customers started calling us to find out where the pharmacy bags were with their advertising on it. They paid for them and rightfully expected to see them!

Neither of us knew what to do. We were so disheartened; I thought I had found a home.

It was in the dead of winter as the business was imploding. I never knew a place could be as cold. One morning I woke up to find my car, which had the parking brake on, had slid all by itself out of the driveway into the middle of the cul-de-sac I lived on.

I pushed it to the curb. When I came back, the car was almost completely buried in ice as a result of the snowplow that had gone through.

When I finally got the car freed, I called my friend who was selling pharmacy bags with me and told him I was sick and tired of living in Omaha and hated the cold weather. He was used to the cold, but he was tired of it as well.

We decided right then and there that we were going to Arizona (where it was warm) to open our own pharmacy bag advertising business. Lack of money always played a part in my decision-making process. With no financial education, poor decisions were always compounded.

Sometimes we are REACTIVE, other times we are CREATIVE. Look closer. Only the "C" has been moved. When you "C" things clearly, you move from being REACTIVE to being CREATIVE!

Off we went, short on cash, but my friend had credit cards. Along the way, I remember stopping to get gas and seeing the steel belts coming out of my tires. We were running pretty thin! But in my heart, I knew I could win with money! I had to … so my mother would be proud of me!

My problem was not that I didn't know how to make money. I did. It's just that I didn't know how to keep it, much less protect and manage it properly.

As a result, I was willing to listen to anyone's advice … regardless of their qualifications. That is not a smart thing to do!

The life lesson I learned:

How much more money would I have today if I had the financial education all my life that I have today? Or how much better would my relationships have been with other people if I would have had the maturity to ask the right questions and to know how to communicate effectively with the opposite sex? One of my biggest goals today is to help young people be financially educated and show them how to effectively communicate with the opposite sex. We could change the world! Divorce rates would drop, there would be fewer "latch key" kids, and we would have much better communication! I had no teachers and I was a terrible student. I didn't even know the right questions to ask! I learned neither of these important lessons until age 44!

FINANCIAL LESSON:

Be careful who you accept advice from! When you accept their advice, be ready to accept their lifestyle! Broke friends are more than willing to tell you how to make money. Listen to them and you will stay broke! People don't want to be part of the process, they just want to be part of the outcome! But the "process" is where you figure out who is entitled to be part of the outcome!

...

NOTES TO SELF:

EIGHTEEN

Going South Again

We stopped and rented an apartment in Scottsdale, Arizona. Both of our families remained behind in Nebraska.

My partner and I both knew how to sell the pharmacy bag advertising program, so the next morning we went to work. I talked to a pharmacy close by, he liked what he heard, and signed an agreement to let us sell advertising on his pharmacy bags.

Our offer was pretty straight forward: We sell advertising and then we pay for the bags and give them to the pharmacy for free. We increased their profit margin by lowering their business costs. They no longer had to buy bags!

It was actually a pretty smart business.

Later, as my friend and I congratulated ourselves on landing our first contract, we both suddenly realized we had a new problem. We had no idea where pharmacy bags came from! Nor did we have a graphic artist who could make the ads!

We scrambled like any entrepreneur and figured it out for ourselves. Mind you, we had no legal counsel, business documentation, or bank accounts, but hey, we were starting to make money!

What put us on the map was a medium-size local drugstore chain with 25 locations. That contract was large enough for us to open an office in Phoenix and start hiring people.

Wisely, we hired two very good telemarketers to help set the appointments. My business partner and I would show up and close the sales. It worked incredibly well, and we were averaging a 60% closing ratio, impressive for any product or service.

One local prospective client was the largest grocery chain in the market. I wanted to get all their pharmacies, as that would add more than 100 stores to our business, but they would never allow me to meet with the corporate buyer.

After countless attempts, I finally reached him! I asked him if he would give me exactly three minutes to hear my proposal. I even said that I would bring a three-minute egg timer and stop when it dinged.

He laughed because of my persistence and agreed to give me an appointment. He liked what he heard, and after a few subsequent committee meetings, we landed the contract for that chain!

Because of the success we were having, we were able to move our families from Nebraska down to Arizona with us. That made life easier for all of us.

The life lesson I learned:

Never give up on your dreams! Remember first, that everything you think, say and do is a reflection of what you've decided about yourself! You are recreating yourself in every moment of NOW!

FINANCIAL LESSON:

Right now, someone far less qualified than you is living *your* dreams! What you *want* shows up in your conversations, but what you *expect* shows up in your *actions!*

...

NOTES TO SELF:

Nineteen

Big Win, Bigger Loss

Our business continued to grow! We hired another telemarketer and a couple of salespeople to go out on appointments. In less than a year we were making about $25,000 dollars per month! Of course, we had overhead as well.

Monumentally, this was the first time in my life that I chose not to spend everything I made. And while I was not really saving much due to the business costs, I was not deep in debt either.

One day, out of the blue, our supplier of pharmacy bags called with bad news. They had run out of the special machine-glazed paper that we needed to use to keep the ink on the bags from bleeding. Without that special paper, we had no bags.

New inventory would arrive in about three months, they said, but that would not work for us.

My partner and I scrambled. We called every supplier we could find, but they all said the same thing. There was no paper in stock.

I called the big corporate buyer, who had been very pleased with us up to that point, and told him what was happening. We had already sold the advertising but could not produce the product. It was not our fault, but it directly affected everyone.

The big corporate buyer even pitched in and tried to use his clout to locate the machine-glazed paper for us, but he had no luck either.

Pharmacies could still use their normal pharmacy bags in the interim, that part was easy. The hard part was the fact that people had purchased advertisements and we were not able to deliver the product within a reasonable amount of time.

It wasn't our fault, but that sounded hollow to the advertiser who bought from us. Their relationship was with us, not the bag supplier.

Many clients wanted their money back. Fortunately, we did gain something from the previous pharmacy bag business! We used the legalese from that sales contract to implement a "no refund" policy in the event something like this happened.

It was very stressful, but we got through it.

Unfortunately, it was four months before the special paper was available. At that point, the cost tripled, and we were out of business.

It was our only product and without it, we had no revenue, employees, sales reps, or office building ... we had nothing.

Here I was, broke again, but this time I was not that deep in debt. As a result, it was much easier to survive.

My business partner found a job selling cars at a local dealership. While I didn't have any interest in selling cars, I needed to do something for cash flow, so I joined him. I only lasted four months. To me, I felt like I was always trying to get more money out of people when they purchased a car, and I knew they couldn't afford it.

Imagine my surprise when one day the phone rang, it was an old colleague of mine who said an Australian-based company was looking for a corporate president for their US division and he recommended me. Was I open to listening to their offer? You bet; I was!

They wanted me to relocate to Orange County, California and the offer was $85,000 salary to start, a company car of my choosing (within reason), an expense account, 401K, health insurance and nice trips to Australia and New Zealand.

Make it one of your daily affirmations to create wealth.

One other person was being considered. Since he was from Australia, I had the advantage.

I negotiated a better deal than they were offering, which was exciting. I finally held out for something I wanted instead of giving in to what someone else wanted. The salary I requested and received was $102,000! I had finally achieved a six-figure annual income after 18 years in corporate America! I was so excited, but I didn't realize the real price I would have to pay in the other parts of my life!

It was a wild ride, to say the least. I dropped everything I was doing and moved to a place in Huntington Beach. Think of it as today's Airbnb. I rented a bedroom and bathroom from a guy, and we shared the rest of the house.

Finding furnishings and a new office building was the first priority. I also had to procure warehouse space for a lot of products, and then a lot of employees.

My wife came out to look at homes but ultimately decided that California wasn't for her. She knew I needed this job, so the family stayed in Phoenix. I flew to join them every weekend, from Friday night to Monday morning, and then I worked like crazy all week at the new California offices.

With my six-figure income, I was not going into debt, but the travel and lifestyle pretty much absorbed all our monthly income.

It's what I call, "being broke at a higher-level."

The company I worked for had divisions in 32 other countries, but of those, only five were profitable. My division was one of those five, that made money.

Unbeknownst to me, the owner was starting to pull funds from the profitable divisions to offset losses of other divisions. He never told us, but when our corporate checks started bouncing, we quickly found out! We didn't have online banking back in those days, so we didn't know our full financial predicament until we received our monthly bank statement.

By then, it was too late. Checks were bouncing all over the place. I called the owner and said I could not do anything else until this was corrected. He said he would get back to me. Two weeks later he did … by telling me that they were closing the company worldwide!

They owed me $40,000, but I would never see a penny of it.

The life lesson I learned:

Don't do something permanently stupid just because you're temporarily upset! There are over seven and a half billion people in the world! Are you going to let one of them ruin you?

FINANCIAL LESSON:

Even though you may be making good money at your *job*, someone else has control of everything. You truly have no control, only responsibility! The grass isn't greener on the other side, it's only greener where you water it!

...

NOTES TO SELF:

TWENTY

Coming Up Empty

My life felt like a broken record! I was facing unemployment yet again! Only this time, I was not as deep in debt.

To put food on the table, I started sacking groceries at the local grocery store and throwing a paper route. It was hard to believe after a six-figure income that I was in this position!

This was ridiculous! I was 44 years old! I had relocated 11 times in 20 years for corporate jobs. But here I was! How could it be? I had done all the things I thought were right … I started in an entry-level sales position with the Pillsbury Company and ended up being a corporate president for the US division of an International Company.

In spite of my success, I was still unemployed, broke, and bagging groceries!

After 20 years of climbing the corporate ladder, what did I really have? I had 20 years of experience, but no cash flow!

It was past time for some serious self-evaluation! A lot of my friends called it my "mid-life crisis," but I call it my "mid-life review!"

A few weeks after the company closed down, I took a ring to a local jeweler to get it fixed. The jeweler said he could fix it. Instead, he ruined it!

I confronted him; our conversation did not go well. He refused to make any restitution! I left extremely frustrated.

Accept the right philosophy about money! Create a personal budget and eliminate BAD debt.

It's with great emphasis that I say how fortunate I am that this happened. As I walked angrily away from the jewelry store, I remembered the "legal thing" I had bought a couple of months earlier. It was a monthly subscription service, and one of the benefits of the membership was that it allowed me to call a law firm in my state and get legal advice without worrying about getting a bill.

There I was, treated so unfairly, but with the ability to call a law firm without the fear of getting a bill! I called them immediately and ended up speaking with a female attorney about my jewelry problem.

The life lesson I learned:

If you ever have a jewelry problem, get a female attorney.

FINANCIAL LESSON:

Learn to master money so the *lack* of money doesn't master you!

...

NOTES TO SELF:

TWENTY-ONE

Finding a Gem

The attorney was very professional and thorough. She spent about 45 minutes asking me questions about what happened? She wanted to know about the ring, the costs, the promises, etc. I never got a bill for that call.

Then she called the jeweler on my behalf and told him what my rights were as a consumer.

I never got a bill for that call either. What I did get was a check from the jeweler for $2,152.32 to replace the ring!

My low monthly legal membership subscription was outrageously valuable at that point! I was blown away! And his bank gladly cashed the check for me. As I stood in the bank lobby with the money in my hands, I thought to myself, "How many times have I gone through frustrating experiences where I felt like I was being treated unfairly?"

I could have used that legal service a lot of times over the years!

It was at that moment that I became a "product of the product."

When I got home, I called the person I had bought the membership from and asked what he did for a living. He simply said, "We show people information, then we let them get their questions answered. When they buy it, we get paid!"

With my professional background, and a very real need to generate income, I asked him questions about quotas, time commitments, and commissions. He told me it would be my business and that I could do it spare-time, part-time, or full-time. He was also doing the business part-time, so he said my questions would be best answered by someone else. He and I then had a three-way call with a guy who happened to be the #1 money earner in the company.

After a couple of questions, he stopped me and said, "Larry, you've already received a check for over $2000! You've already become a product of the product. Instead of trying to piece this all together, why don't you come to one of our live events and take a full look at the information? That way you can make an intelligent decision. Whichever way you decide to go, that's fine. It's up to you."

That made total sense, and I liked it being "up to me."

The life lesson I learned:

If it's important, you'll find a way! If it's not, you'll find an excuse!

FINANCIAL LESSON:

Sometimes when you have an internal feeling that something is too good to be true, but you believe in your heart it's right, you *must* act on it! Fear in most cases is simply being uneducated on the subject matter, whether it's investing or making money!

...

NOTES TO SELF:

TWENTY-TWO

Still Dreaming?

To my chagrin, the live event I had been invited to was in Orlando, Florida, completely on the opposite side of the country. It was also only a week away!

So, I maxed out a credit card to get to that event. The guy I bought the membership from picked me up at the airport and took me to the venue. There were 188 people in the room, and I sat on the second row. It was not fancy at all. There was no PowerPoint presentation or a slick movie. We sat on metal fold-up chairs and there was a whiteboard on a tripod in the front.

If you want to succeed, you must first improve. But in order to improve, you must first practice. The only way you can practice is to learn. But in order to learn, you must first fail. When you first started riding a bicycle, how many times did you get back up after falling? Today, you could ride a bike in your sleep.

When they introduced the speaker, it was the same #1 money earner who had talked with me a week earlier. They announced that he was earning more than a million dollars per year!

I was skeptical immediately! I could feel myself starting to shut down. After all, I had spent 20 years in corporate America and had never made a million dollars cumulatively!

How on earth could he be making over a million dollars PER YEAR? To boot, he only started his business three years prior!

The life lesson I learned:

Don't let small minds convince you that your dreams are too big!

FINANCIAL LESSON:

I'd rather be curious and wealthy instead of skeptical and broke!

...

NOTES TO SELF:

TWENTY-THREE

Recipe for Success

I stayed to listen because I'd already paid for the ticket and the hotel room, but I was brooding in skepticism.

The #1 earner stood in front of the room with only a black and white brochure, telling everyone about the credibility of the company, the services they offered, the compensation opportunity for those who had an interest in earning more income, and the timing behind the company.

After his brief, but thorough, presentation, it all made total sense to me. It really did! I also had cashed a check for over $2,000 as living proof that it worked. The membership cost $25 a month, and the amount I got back from the jeweler paid for more than seven years of my monthly subscription cost!

It hit me, at that moment … If the membership subscription was a no brainer to me, then it might be to other people as well!

I thought to myself, "If the membership made sense and it was affordable to pretty much anyone … and all I had to do was show it to others, and let them get their questions answered … and then I just allowed them to make an informed decision just like I had … and if they bought it, I would get paid!"

Made sense to me!

After the meeting was over, the #1 money earner and a few other people invited me for a bite to eat. At the dinner table, I asked him how he could make over a million dollars marketing a $25 service!

He said there were only five simple keys to success in the business. He explained, counting on one hand,

1. 15 minutes
2. Show
3. You may or may not be interested
4. Two a day
5. A weekly meeting

I had no idea what he was talking about, but it seemed pretty simple. Five short secrets to success couldn't be all that hard to grasp.

He unraveled the five secrets in a quick explanation:

> "When you approach someone, don't assault them. Ask if they have about 15 minutes, tell them there is something important you want to show them, and tell them they may or may not be interested. Do two presentations like that every day and attend one weekly meeting."

That was it! Both the approach and philosophy made sense to me. It didn't feel like I would need to force anyone to buy anything. So, I agreed to give it a go!

Pay yourself first.

As soon as I was back in California, I shared the opportunity with my friend and former work associate who served as the VP of the Australian based company. He was in need of a way to earn a good income!

He listened and "got it," as I had. He was my first business associate and member!

Back then, everything was done by snail mail. I put my associate agreement, his associate agreement, and his membership agreement in the same envelope.

The cost to start the business (and become an associate) was $49. I didn't have $49 liquid at that point. I had been unemployed for a few weeks and was taking on debt again, so I wrote a hot check for $49 and included it in the envelope.

A few days later I received my first commission check for $62.50 ... and promptly ran to the bank to deposit it! Thankfully, my $49 check didn't bounce! They were slower depositing my check than I was depositing theirs!

From that point forward, I went to work doing exactly what the #1 money earner had told me to do. His five simple keys to success worked brilliantly.

Within 90 days, I was making $1,000 per week and I was still only part-time, working about 10 hours per week.

I began to learn the power of leveraged income.

The life lesson I learned:

A mastermind group is a peer-to-peer mentoring concept used to help members

solve their problems with input and advice from the other group members. The concept was coined in 1925 by author Napoleon Hill in his book *The Law of Success* and described in more detail in his 1937 book, *Think and Grow Rich*. But if you use this mastermind concept in school, it's called "cheating!" Remember the Evolution of a Belief System at the beginning of the book? This is a great example!

Financial Lesson:

When you listen to people who already have the lifestyle you want and you take action, you can start making money! Remember, if you accept their advice, be prepared to accept their lifestyle!

...

Notes to Self:

TWENTY-FOUR

Starting Over

The company's big national convention was coming up, but I was still trying to play catch-up financially. Luckily, I found a way to attend! I was so determined to be there, I slept in a sleeping bag on the floor of another representative's hotel room!

I had no money to eat out. I took a backpack filled with water bottles, granola bars, and peanuts.

I was very impressed with everything I saw. My experience with the jeweler helped to cement my belief in the service. It was the fact that I could actually make money by referring the service to others that was a stretch for my mind.

Set financial goals and evaluate your achievements against those goals every day, every week, every month, and every year!

When the founder of the company completed the convention with his keynote speech, I was all in! I was committed!

As soon as I got back home, I went full-time with my new home-based business. And by my ninth month ... I was making more money each month than I ever had in all 20 years in Corporate America!

I was finally starting to get ahead financially. Admittedly, if I had learned and gained an ounce of financial education, I would've had money in the bank from my first job. It felt like I was starting over, because I was.

The life lesson I learned:

Nobody else is going to take care of you financially except you!

FINANCIAL LESSON:

No matter how much money you make, pay yourself first. If you took ten cents out of every dollar and stored it for yourself in a "financial freedom" account, and do it starting right now, you will be surprised what time will do for you and your money!

...

NOTES TO SELF:

TWENTY-FIVE

Dream Income

In the second year of my home-based business, I made $224,000! My income was more than double any salary I'd ever earned working for others.

Two years compared to 20-years; it really wasn't a fair comparison! What was the difference between 20 years in corporate America compared to two years of having my own home-based business?

How did a high school dropout with a GED and no college education, double his highest corporate salary in only two years?

Build a 6 to 12-month emergency fund that will roll over into your investment (financial freedom) account.

You have to be wondering what made my home-based business work so well? I brought the same work ethic and work discipline to my own home-based business as I had in my corporate jobs. I had never been afraid to pour myself into anything that was legitimate and made money.

After two decades in corporate with repeated periods of unemployment, I learned a very important lesson! The difference wasn't me – the difference was the opportunity.

Sadly, my wife was done with the relocations, changes, and instability, and we were both tired of arguing over the disagreements! We divorced. I felt like such a failure in life, even though I was having success in business! Looking back, I see my inability to communicate well as a major factor in the demise of my personal relationships. Since then, I've worked hard on myself to correct these foundational issues and I'm happy to say that today I can resolve conflict and articulate my feelings in a meaningful way.

The life lesson I learned:

The older you get; the faster time seems to fly! Every year is important to your future! Don't waste any more time no matter what age you are!

FINANCIAL LESSON:

"Pay your bills with job income. Start your fortune income part-time! When your part-time fortune income passes your job income, quit your job and create your fortune!"

– Jim Rohn

...

NOTES TO SELF:

TWENTY-SIX

Out of the Race

Through my home-based business, I learned that there are other types of income, such as leveraged override income and residual income! Both were new to me, but neither had ever been an option before. All I knew about was linear income; trading time for money!

How many times in your life have you ever been paid over and over again for something you did one time? That doesn't happen very often, does it?

Practically speaking, if you quit your job today, how long would they continue to pay you? Even though you worked hard and did great things for your company, would they continue to pay you if you quit the company? I can't think of a single company that would do that, if there is not residual income involved.

For 20 years in corporate America, all I really did was exchange time for money. If I did not work; I did not get paid. If I got sick more than the few days that were allowed each year, I didn't get paid. If I wanted to vacation more than the small amount of time that corporate America gave me, my choices were either not to get paid, or to be fired!

(Note: This year, my wife and I, will spend more than 110 days on vacation: Maui twice, Vail, New York City, Vegas, Sonoma County, Lake Chapala in Mexico, Denver twice, Balboa Island in CA, San Diego, Palm Beach/Jensen Beach, Lake Dora, Cabo San Lucas, Vancouver, BC, Malta, and Sicily, Italy. That's not the lifestyle I was offered in corporate.)

Entrepreneurship is living a few years like most people won't, so that you can live the rest of your life like most people can't.

Without question, all I was really doing in corporate jobs was building someone else's dream at the expense of my own. THAT idea of the American Dream isn't so dreamy.

Over the years, I heard rumors about leveraged income and residual income and the "so-called" worst business of all ... network marketing! Many people, including some of my family members, called it a pyramid scheme.

After four and a half years of running my own home-based business, my cumulative personal income was more than one million dollars! It wasn't a million dollars per year like the #1 earner in the company, but what I made in my first four and a half years was way beyond any income I could have earned in corporate. After all, I hadn't made one million dollars cumulatively in two full decades of corporate jobs!

Sadly, my success made a few of my friends very uncomfortable. Some of them actually started telling people that I was about to go to prison for fraud!

Today, some of those same people sit in rush hour traffic twice a day and work jobs where other people call all the shots. They live paycheck to paycheck and keep adding to their credit card debt.

Not me, I'm done with that. I used to live that life, but thankfully I was able to get out

The life lesson I learned:

"You can have everything in life you want if you will just help other people get what they want," as Zig Ziglar used to say.

FINANCIAL LESSON:

"Ordinary" is getting dressed in clothes you bought for work and driving through traffic in a car you still owe money on… in order to get to the job you need to pay for the clothes and the car and the house you leave vacant all day long so you can afford to live in it! "Extra ordinary" therefore is *not* doing this. Which—*ordinary* or *extra ordinary*—do you prefer?

…

NOTES TO SELF:

TWENTY-SEVEN

Freedom Defined

It's incredible to hear some of the excuses I get when I share the concept of a home-based business. Some people say they don't want to have their own business because they don't want to pay their own taxes. Maybe they think it's difficult to do or that they will have less actual income as a result?

Here is the bottom line! You get the freedom that comes with being your own boss, an unlimited earning potential that depends on your own commitment level, (not your boss's opinion of what you're worth), your team's commitment level and hard work - and you have the opportunity to pay less real tax dollars, than the person stuck behind a desk who seldom gets a raise!

Being a W-2 employee does not allow you to write off authorized IRS tax deductions for your business expenses.

Of course, paying more or less in taxes doesn't make people good or bad/right or wrong! It simply means they are paying more money in taxes than they need to.

If you are employed with W-2 income, taxes are taken out of your hourly wage or your salary based on how much money you make.

Makes sense, right? That's how it works.

But when you are self-employed, you are allowed to take authorized tax deductions from the IRS, which simply means you can pay less money in taxes. Now don't get me wrong, I am all about paying my fair share of taxes, but I certainly don't want to overpay!

Being self-employed provides tax privileges that W-2 employees do not get, period!

Here is a real example:

> In one of my recent tax returns, I would have paid roughly $141,805 in taxes for the year had I been a W-2 employee. But because I was paid as an independent contractor (1099 rather than W-2), I paid $73,088 in taxes.

My home-based business is structured properly as an S Corp, and I have a great accountant and tax attorney. In total, I paid $68,717 less in taxes because my business expenses actually lowered my taxable income.

This never happens when you're an employee. Your salary is your taxable income and your only deductions are the standard ones offered by the IRS.

See the difference? I'll further illustrate it!

The tax on my reduced self-employed income was $73,088, while the taxes on the full amount as an employee with W2 income would have been roughly $141,805! The difference is $68,717 that I did not have to pay in taxes.

I'm not saying you should run out and join a network marketing company. What you do to build passive income is up to you. For me, this is the best vehicle I have personally found to capitalize on the two things I want most in life, not including, of course, my spiritual desires:

1. *TIME*
2. *MONEY*

Create income-producing assets so you can generate passive income. It's the very best kind … money that comes in whether you work or not. Remember, if it doesn't PAY YOU, it's NOT an asset!

I think most people want these same things because when combined they give you FREEDOM! A lot of people have time, but no money. Vice versa, some people have money and no time. Very few people have both.

Below is the best definition of the freedom that I speak of.

> *Freedom is being able to do what you want, when you want, where you want, with whoever you want, for as long as you want, without having to worry about money!*

That's the very type of freedom I have found. It's also the same type of freedom that most people want!

I chose to work with a company that allowed me to create my fortune. There were no quotas, which meant I could work in my spare-time, part-time, or full time. The company sells a service, not a product. A lot of people love to sell, but not everyone understands the power of leveraged income. The nicest thing about our service is we can go to companies and offer it as an employee benefit because of the incredible value proposition.

The residual income in my business can be willed to my family when I pass. Leaving a legacy for the ones I love remains exceptionally important to me. I read in a good book that said, "A good man will leave an inheritance for his children's children."

I do want to state that not all network marketing companies are created equal. As with any type of business, there are good and bad. I worked for both good and bad companies in corporate.

The networking marketing company I chose to work with pays every day, Monday through Friday. That means fast cash flow. Cash flow was extremely important when I started because I was hurting financially. The low cost of entry also helped.

The opportunity along with the financial knowledge I've gained has allowed me to help others create six-figure incomes, and a few have even become millionaires! Not everyone achieves that level, but the opportunity is there.

How many 'jobs' give you the opportunity to become a millionaire?

Hoping to become millionaires, Larry Smith and John Blalack show off the money they've earned shing shoes. They spit shine shoes for 50 cents a pair and boots for $2.00 a pair. John and Larry have handled nearly 100 pairs of shoes in the three weeks they've been in business. These two hope to stay in business all year; think about them when Federal shoe-shine time arrives.

Above all this, I've learned the value of mentorship! I've been able to meet, work, socialize, travel the world, and hang out with people whose mindsets have helped me become a better person all the way around!

Again, I'm not saying you need to choose the industry I chose. I'm simply sharing with you why I chose it!

Freedom is not about becoming a millionaire or amassing as much money as possible. Once you have freedom, the question then becomes:

"Now that money is not an issue, what are you going to do? What is your passion?"

When you were young, didn't you ponder that question? We all did. We dreamed about what we wanted to do and be when we grew up.

But at a certain point, we stopped dreaming and …

- put our heads down and joined the rat race

- climbed the corporate ladder
- competed with everyone else
- looked forward to retirement

Whatever your age, why not carve out a few hours per week and figure out how to monetize your passion? Pay your bills from job income and create your fortune part-time.

Who knows where that will lead you!

The life lesson I learned:

People often forget that it's our choice HOW we want to spend the rest of our lives!

FINANCIAL LESSON:

Why wouldn't you have a business of your own if it helps you ultimately to increase your wealth? What do you love doing? How do you create your own business out of it? Start part-time and supplement your income. Dedicate yourself to it and watch what can happen to your financial future! You are capable of *anything* you put your mind to!

...

NOTES TO SELF:

TWENTY-EIGHT

Time Crunch

How do you spend your extra time? By "extra" I mean all the time you aren't at work or in bed sleeping.

How many hours are spent in front of the television each week? Or bouncing around in all the social media platforms that are out there these days? Or reading fiction books?

What if you could spend 5-10 hours per week building something for you, your family, and your family's financial legacy?

There are 168 hours in every week. Let's say you sleep 8 hours per night, that's 56 hours.

Let's say you work 40 hours per week with an hour in the morning and an hour in the evening commuting back and forth. That's another 10 hours per week.

168 hours per week

Sleep = 56 hours
Work = 40 hours
Commuting = 10 hours
Total hours spent = 106

That leaves 62 hours each week to do whatever you want.

That breaks down to be almost nine hours per day.

62 hours free / 7 days a week

Free time per day = almost 9 hours

CREDIT CARDS: PART 1 OF 2

Some suggest paying off high interest credit cards before you save. This is because interest rates on credit cards are higher than what savings vehicles are paying. This makes financial sense, but sometimes it's more about creating habits to get to your financial goals!

LET ME SAY IT AGAIN!

After work, sleep and commuting, you have almost nine hours PER DAY left over! That's a lot of time to do something to bring you financial profit and freedom!

Yes, I know, there is a myriad of other tasks that need to be completed in that same timeframe. We have to grocery shop, do laundry, cook, clean, help children with homework or attend events. Still, with ALL that keeps us busy, there IS time left to work on something productive and profitable.

Most employees don't stop to add up the amount of time they spend in traffic. Have you ever done it?

If you spend an hour in the morning and an hour in the evening driving to and from work, that is no less than 10 hours per week or 40 hours per month.

This equates to working one additional WEEK each month just to go back and forth to work so you can make money!

Add in the cost of fuel, now you are spending money to make money. How much do you spend on food at restaurants, clothes, dry cleaners, and daycare, all because of your job?

Have you ever added up all these expenses and subtracted it from what you bring home from your job each month?

That amount is your actual net income.

Do you know what your net income truly is? I'm not talking about the net income from your paycheck! I'm talking about the net income from your job after you pay all the expenses to have the job! That's a totally different number!

If you have never stopped to calculate your net income, you should do it. The amount might amaze you!

Here's how you calculate it on a monthly basis:

Gross Income:
Net Income (after taxes):
Clothes for work:
Gas for the car for work:
Time in traffic going to and from work (based on your average hourly/salary rate):
Daycare:
Lunch money:
Happy Hour or after-work social gatherings:
Any miscellaneous expenses:
Actual Net Income:

Could you make less money in a home-based business and actually net as much or more money than you do in your job? That's another important question to answer.

Who would be controlling your time if you run your own business? Not your employer! It would be you.

Despite the solid mathematical evidence, factoring in commuting, and the reality of net income, I find people who still tell me they don't have an extra 5-10 hours per week to create their freedom!

That's in a whole week!

Don't allow yourself to say, "I don't have the time." Everybody has the exact same amount of time in a day, week, month, and year! Why is it then that some people seem to accomplish amazing things while others seem to struggle? It's all based on your priorities and what's important to you!

If you really want to examine yourself:

- Track each day for one week
- List how you spent each 24 hours
- Be truthful with yourself

You will see how you are actually spending your time!

The fact is, there are so many ways you can create new money without having another job, and without having to leave your job! Again, pay your bills with job income and create your fortune part-time!

Here's a great example, we recently had some rooms in our house painted. The painter brought his son to help and I began to ask the 18-year-old questions about what he did.

CREDIT CARDS: PART 2 OF 2

If you use all your money to pay off credit cards and have no emergency fund (investment account), when an emergency comes up (it always will), you'll have to put the new expense on a credit card. Create the habit of paying yourself FIRST and then pay off your credit card debt. The

"you-first" habit is the most important habit of all!

He explained how he had a full-time job, but in his spare time, he sold things online. He told me how he goes to local flea markets, garage sales, and thrift stores to buy goods at a discount. Then he sells them online and makes a profit.

Instead of going out partying or playing video games, this young man took his spare time and put it to work. He created a business of his own completely on the side. He has his priorities in order, and if he stays with it, one day he will have a life that most people dream about.

This is why personal development plays such an important role in our lives! Success is something that you attract by the person you become!

Remember, everything you've ever wanted is on the other side of FEAR!

The life lesson I learned:

Everything in life is based on how we think! Do you have a "growth" mindset or a "fixed" mindset? You are capable of amazing things!

GROWTH MINDSET -VS- FIXED MINDSET:

I can learn anything I want to -vs-
I'm either good at it or I'm not.

When I'm frustrated, I persevere -vs-
When I'm frustrated, I give up.

I want to challenge myself -vs-
I don't like to be challenged.

When I fail, I learn -vs-
When I fail, I'm no good.

Tell me I try hard -vs-
Tell me I'm smart.

If you succeed, I'm inspired -vs-
If you succeed, I feel threatened.

My effort & attitude determine everything
-vs-
My abilities determine everything.

TWENTY-NINE

Keep Reaching

Often, people will build up enough courage to step out of their comfort zone, only to be frightened right back in, due to fear!

I've heard so many reasons why people say they can't start a business. Here are just a few:

- **No time** – But we all have the same amount of time.
- **No money** – How many years have you been working? If you don't have any money, I can't think of a better reason to start your own business!

- **No experience** – So invest your time and learn how to turn your passion into a business!

In spite of my encouragement, some people will even argue, "I don't see how you can go to work every day **NOT knowing** how much money you're going to make!"

My response is, I don't see how you can go to work every day **KNOWING how much** money you're going to make!

It's not meant to be insulting. The truth is, they have no opportunity to change their hourly rate, or their salary on a daily basis. When you create an opportunity outside of that box, you can change your circumstances.

Still, my question is, why can't you have both?

KNOW how much money you are going to make, and with your part-time business add to the amount of money you KNOW you are going to make!

That's why I started my business part-time! I needed to build an investment account to create multiple streams of income, and I didn't have any money to do it with because of my lack of financial education!

Your mindset determines everything! This is why I suggest starting part time! You can add more money to your household. For peace of mind, don't put your current income in jeopardy!

Maybe it's the fear of rejection, fear of success, fear of failure, fear of having more money than you know what to do with, fear of running out of money, or even fear of ridicule from your friends and family that hold you back?

Fear of ridicule from friends and family? Sounds silly, right? It happens more than you might think!

You might be wondering, "Wait, how could friends and family do that to someone? I mean, why would they ridicule someone for wanting a better way of life? They should be supportive!"

You are right, they should be supportive, but it is not always the case!

People who say it can't be done, shouldn't interrupt those that are doing it.

People will reach out to try something new, but if they don't have immediate success, they often shrink back to whatever they were previously doing ... knowing full well that it will NOT give them their lifelong dream. They know it won't work, but they keep at it. If you were that consistent with your DREAM, it WOULD work!

Please understand that I'm not judging anyone for their choices, I made poor ones for years! **I'm simply Daring You to Get Rich, in hopes you'll catch on sooner than I did.**

After more than two decades of running my own business, I've seen people from every walk of life find the success they are looking for. Success is not impossible!

You name it, I've seen it. From single moms to married women with kids, from GEDs (like mine) to PHDs, from people who have gone bankrupt (like me) to multi-millionaires, from doctors to the homeless, I've seen them be incredibly successful in their own business.

I've also seen these same types of people experience failure. They failed, not because their business didn't work, but because they gave up!

In 2013, entrepreneur Jamie Siminoff appeared on the popular TV show, Shark Tank. He was there to show off his product: Ring Doorbell. All five of the Sharks turned him down.

Did he give up? Did he throw in the towel? Not at all! He stayed committed to his dream and just five short years later, Jamie sold his company for more than one billion dollars!

One thing is for sure, that never would have happened if he had given up on his dream.

Quitting is the only sure way to fail.

Harland C. Stonecipher, a man I have respected for more than 24 years, used to say, "Not all dreams come true! But dreams never dreamed will never come true! So, dream bigger!"

Excellent advice!

The life lesson I learned:

Right now, start where you are! Don't make excuses! Start NOW: TODAY! It's your life and only YOU can control what happens with it. Start with fear, doubt, and pain, but just start! Start and don't stop! Remember, I didn't "start" until age 44!

FINANCIAL LESSON:

The best way to predict your future is to *create* it!

...

NOTES TO SELF:

THIRTY

The Dough Boy

Let's get a little more personal and talk about life for a minute.

- What does your life look like?
- How do you spend Monday through Friday?

If you didn't do the exercise from before and write down your daily routine on a piece of paper, I challenge you to do it now.

Once you've written out what your days look like, all 24 hours of them, then answer these questions as well:

- Does your day inspire you?
- Do you wake up every morning looking forward to your day?
- Do you find yourself always looking forward to the weekends?
- If so, why shouldn't every day be a "weekend day" ... where you always call the shots?
- Do you ever wake up thinking about a lack of money or bills?
- How much of your life has been drained by thinking about 'lack of money'?
- How much stress has a lack of money caused in your life?

I ask you to close your eyes for 30 seconds. I want you to dream about a life where "money" was NEVER, EVER a part of your thought process! How much more empowering would your life be? Could you help to make a difference in other peoples' lives, because you weren't stressed about your own situation!

Here is an even bigger question:

> Why do you let someone else dictate your life 5 or 6 days out of 7? That translates into over 71% or 85% of your week ... your life ... your living?

Sure, there are a lot of justifiable reasons why people get into a routine and stay at a job they have, but take a moment and decide if you truly want to stay where you are. Remember, you don't have to leave your 'bill paying job'. Start your fortune income part time! You have the time if you make it a priority!

Do you really want to go through life with constant negative thoughts of money on your mind? Hasn't' it drained enough of your time already?

As a teenager and into my young adulthood, my mother told me over and over, "Larry, you'll never turn out to be anything!" Those words crushed me! I always felt like a failure. I had a **fixed mindset** at that age.

As an adult today with a **growth mindset**, I better understand what was really taking place. She was parenting the best way she knew how. She saw more in me than I saw in myself! What she was really voicing was her frustration that I wouldn't stick with anything long enough to master it.

Sure, I was good at a lot of things, but never pursued any of them long enough to be great.

I believe she was trying to inspire me to become all that I was meant to be. She was right, I was not living up to my potential!

But as a young person, all I heard was ***what she said*** and not ***what she meant***. As a result, I had a burning desire to prove her wrong and show her that I could do whatever I wanted to do. I simply needed the right opportunity.

I felt like it finally happened for the first time when I landed a job with Pillsbury at age 25. Once I was there, I worked hard to for a promotion, so I could prove myself to her. I wanted her to be proud of me!

Thankfully, we had a chance to talk. She and her 5th husband came to Houston for my 29th birthday. That day, she told me how proud she was of me and how special my children were to her. Those words were music to my heart and soul!

BE FINANCIALLY FREE: PART 1 OF 2

Pick a comfortable way of life and don't live based on what you make. If $5,000 per month is comfortable, then live on that. When you make more, push all that extra money into your investment account. The more you do that, the quicker you will create more assets to generate passive income.

She also informed me that she was putting me back in her will. She removed me after our Larry's Liquors fiasco. Her husband already made that change in his will. She needed a little time to update hers. Sadly, two months later, they were both dead.

I could have stayed forever at Pillsbury. It was tempting to never look up. It was a great company, offered good benefits, and paid very well. Why would I want to leave something like that?

It all depends on your values.

Here is a different way to think about it. I was making a small amount of money before Pillsbury hired me. Suddenly I felt like a millionaire at age 25 with my salary, company car, expense account, 401K, and health insurance plan. I was thrilled, but as you know, I had zero financial education!

Armed with a ***money mindset,*** if a re-do from 1975 were possible, I would have approached their job offer with skepticism. After all, I knew nothing about the Pillsbury company except for their Pillsbury Doughboy mascot.

Why would they want to hire me and pay me a lot of money when I didn't know a single thing about their company? But all I saw was a solid paycheck with benefits, so I jumped at the chance.

Yet I watch people who are skeptical about starting their own business! Why? You learned the skills for your job, whether it was through education or on the job knowledge. But no matter how you look at it, you learned how to do your job, didn't you? So why couldn't you learn how to build your own business and create time and financial freedom?

Remember, if your job paid you what you were really worth, the company you work for would not make a profit! Because they make money "off of you!" If they couldn't profit off your work, you would not be employed long!

So how does that feel? Knowing that you'll never be paid what you're really worth? Today the words 'job security' are an oxymoron! There is no such thing as job security, so why wouldn't you want to create your *own security* by doing something you love in a business of your own?

BE FINANCIALLY FREE: PART 2 OF 2

The more assets you have that spin-off passive income, the less you have to work! With enough passive income to cover your obligations, you no longer have to work and you have TIME and MONEY which help you create FREEDOM!

All my friends back then joked and called me the Pillsbury Doughboy. They would poke me in the belly, I would giggle, and they would laugh.

It's funny because today I'm still known as the "Doughboy," though it's a different kind of dough!

The life lesson I learned:

In school, we're taught a lesson and then given a test! In life, we're given a test that teaches us a lesson!

FINANCIAL LESSON:

If you are working on your financial freedom, be willing to ask the tough questions. People with multiple streams of income work on answering those questions every single day!

...

NOTES TO SELF:

THIRTY-ONE

Putting Money in Order

People often reject the idea of creating a home-based business. Some have even asked me, "Why would I pay to have a job?"

They see business expenses and certain costs as a crazy notion. What they don't realize is just how much they pay every day for their current job!

This sadly shows their lack of financial education. I can empathize, I didn't even start to get a financial clue until the age of 44!

At some point, we all need to learn about money. Regardless of our age, regardless of how we make our income, and regardless of whether we agree on everything, we ALL need to learn.

I read a quote from Billionaire Warren Buffet, whose net worth is said to be around $80 billion, and it said, "If you don't learn how to make money when you're sleeping, you'll work until the day you die!"

Back in 1997, I happened to attend a seminar where the author, Robert Kiyosaki, was talking about his book, *Rich Dad/Poor Dad*. I was completely blown away by how little I knew about money!

Everything he said made so much sense. I bought all his books and audios and studied it like a madman. What grabbed me by the throat was his book, *Cash Flow Quadrant*. It suddenly hit me ... I spent my life on the wrong side of the money equation.

No wonder I was always broke and living paycheck to paycheck.

Today, things are very different. Financial education always begins with the principle of paying yourself first. **You must pay yourself first.**

How do you do that with your own home-based business?

Any money you make from your new business is NEW MONEY. Don't include it in the income that you use to pay bills. Instead, this new money has a single purpose:

Develop assets so you can create your own freedom!

Look into setting up an S Corp and have all of your 1099 income flow into your business checking account. It could also be an LLC, so check with your accountant.

As a part-time business owner, put a percentage into your investment bank account first, creating the habit, then your tax escrow bank account, then your business expense bank account.

Don't use this money for personal expenses. Put all of this money into your investment account, except the amount you need for your tax account and your business expense account. As you continue to educate yourself, you will find where you want to invest.

Once you go *full time* in your own business, consider this:

Emergency Fund/Investment Account:

(once your emergency fund is taken care of, the rest of this will go into your investment account)

Put at least 10% of your new money income into this account and work toward the goal of pushing that up to 50%. This way you have more money to invest and create multiple streams of income through investing.

Depending on your age, you may want to limit your riskier or more speculative investments. The older you are, the lower the percentage you may want to risk. Currently, 40% of our 1099 income goes into our investment account.

Get Your Finances in Order

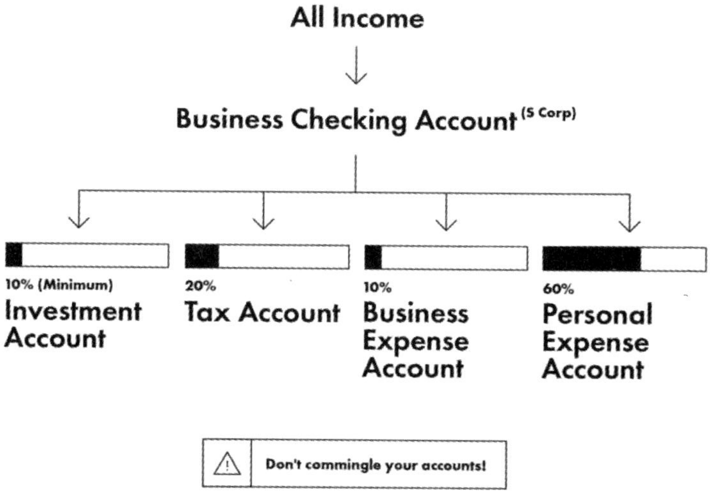

Tax Account:

Make sure you set aside money, 20% will probably do it, to cover your taxes. Tax Day on April 15th always comes! And when it does, you don't want to scramble for money to pay the IRS. Have it saved and ready to go. Also, hire a good accountant. And in a perfect world, have a tax attorney as well! Currently, 12% of our 1099 income goes into our tax account which covers our tax payments.

Business Expense Account:

You are going to have expenses for your business, so set aside a full 10% for that. Make sure you visit with your accountant and see where you can take advantage of tax law that legally allows you to lower the amount of taxes you pay. The more authorized tax deductions you have, the better off you could be! This simply lowers your net income and that means you pay fewer dollars in taxes.

Pay your fair share and never try to beat the system (that will only get you in trouble). I have a great agreement with my accountant and my tax attorney. The law allows legitimate deductions and there is a "chalk line" between legitimate and non-legitimate ... I want chalk all over my shoes, but I never want to cross the line! Currently, 22% of our 1099 income goes into our Business Expense Account so we can maximize authorized tax deductions.

Personal Account:

This is where the balance goes, or 60% when you start. Currently, 26% of our 1099 income is going into our personal account, as it only takes 19% to pay our personal obligations.

Once you have these accounts set up, and begin to get a feel for the money flowing into the accounts, you will be surprised at the opportunities that are suddenly in front of you.

Additionally, when you become proficient in tracking your money, amazing things happen. After I filed bankruptcy in 1989, I committed that one day I would have the perfect credit score of 850, and I did it!

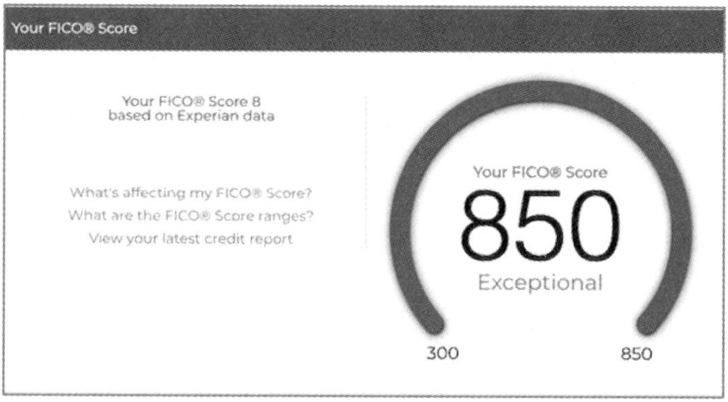

Here is one piece of personal advice, when you give to others less fortunate, money seems to come to you from everywhere! Make this your priority. The gift should come from your personal account. If I had only been this disciplined when I was broke, maybe I would have learned the value of this lesson sooner, too! They say luck is when preparation and opportunity meet up. Organizing and controlling your finances is **preparation**! When opportunities begin to present themselves, your friends will certainly say you are "lucky."

That's fine. You deserve it.

The life lesson I learned:

After being unlucky for 44 years of my life, it was a delight to hear people call me lucky. Those who know the work involved don't call me lucky, but I never mind having to explain what luck really is. Those who understand it are the ones most likely to be lucky themselves!

FINANCIAL LESSON:

A lot of entrepreneurs put all their money into their personal account and then don't have the money necessary for the other payables. Don't do that. Everything you generate in 1099 income is *new* income. Treat it with the respect it deserves.

...

NOTES TO SELF:

THIRTY-TWO

Residual, Passive Income

If you haven't already, it is vitally important that you realize the incredible power of residual, passive income!

As an example, think about this for a minute:

If you were to save money at today's interest rates for CDs, how much money would you need to build a $100,000 residual, passive income every year?

The answer?

Almost $4 million dollars, after taxes.

Of course, you need to know how much that is before taxes because you'll first need to earn it.

The answer?

About $5 million dollars in earned income.

So, in order to make $100,000 every year without lifting a finger, using the interest rates that CDs provide, you will need to earn about $5 million dollars, pay roughly $1 million in taxes, and then you'll have the $100,000 a year in residual, passive income.

Think that will happen? Probably not.

But what if you could build an asset from a home-based business that would generate the same $100,000 per year of residual, passive income?

Why would you NOT invest in a business that could provide this passive income, when you know it's highly unlikely that you'd get it the other way!

Don't count on the government to take care of you! My passive income from my home-based business is regularly more per day than my social security check per month.

Would you do it? Think about how much money you have made in your life up to this point. How much of it is with you right now, liquid cash that you can get your hands on? What percent of the income you have made in your life does your "liquid" income represent? Is that okay? What are you going to do to change that? Remember, *success is a choice!*

For most of us, a lot of money has cumulatively trickled through our fingers. And like sand, it's gone!

Let's be honest:

- How many assets do you have in place?
- What are they paying you?

- Did you think you would be further along financially at this point at your age?

Based on where you are, and then thinking about retirement, how is it looking?

Look at what you have and how many years it has taken you to get to this point. Then figure how much that is per year.

- Will it take you the same number of years to repeat what you have already accomplished?
- And how many more years do you plan to work?
- Where will you be in your savings and investment process at retirement age?

In all honesty, don't you want more?

If that is the case, what are you willing to do about it?

The life lesson I learned:

With some effort, we can create anything and everything. With some effort, we can literally change our lives and become all that we have dreamed of becoming if we choose to do it.

FINANCIAL LESSON:

Create the split-second discipline to track your money. Use financial software so you know where every penny goes. I use Quicken and have for over twenty years. It also saves a lot of time with tax preparation. Remember, knowing where every penny goes will help you tremendously in ways to see how you can further fund your investment account!

...

NOTES TO SELF:

THIRTY-THREE

Life Lessons

One of the most valuable lessons life has taught me is the absolute need for a strong life partner, if you elect to have one.

The challenge is finding that person AND becoming that person for someone else! I say 'becoming' because life is constant change, even in relationships! You have to become that person every day!

When we are young, some of us simply don't have the wisdom to know what questions to ask of the other person. Our youth and exuberance for the attraction we feel often leave us forgetting to ask very important questions. Some of us aren't even self-aware enough to know the questions to ask! Some of these questions would be:

- What do they do for fun?
- Do they want children, and if so, how many?
- What are their financial values?
- What is their credit score? (Yes, that's a great question!)
- What are their spiritual values?
- Do they want to relocate if opportunities come up?
- Do they want to stay in their hometown forever?
- Do they want you both to work?
- What if one has a great job and that requires the other one to leave their job because of relocation?

All of these things, and so much more, are very important to find the right person. While some people have been blessed to have great parents who stayed together, and are great role models in all things, most people haven't experienced this. I sure didn't. Although, as I'm reading the final edit of this book before it goes to proof, we are in Maui, Hawaii. We ran across friends of ours who we joined for dinner. Their parents were with them. They were celebrating their anniversary! They have been married for 57 years! I told them immediately I wanted to set up an interview with them! What wisdom we could learn!

I learned a lot about what NOT to do because of all that life has thrown at me. Trust me, I've made my share of mistakes! After my divorce, I planned to never marry again. In 1998, I happened to meet a young lady at a convention. We became great friends and we stayed friends for years. Only later did we start dating.

When you are with someone you really enjoy, you can have great conversations. See if you have the same mindset and values about life, (because you learned the right questions to ask) and if you do, you can easily become attracted to each other!

We took the time to get to know one another. Ultimately, we got married, and she brought two more beautiful children into my life. Not only is Donielle my best friend, but she has also been a mentor to me in my business and my personal life. She's an amazing woman and so much fun to be around. Together, we have taken our businesses to an entirely new level.

Truly, she is my Proverbs 31 wife! It's a long verse, but includes, "A wife of noble character who can find? She is worth far more than rubies. Her husband has full confidence in her and lacks nothing of value. She brings him good, not harm, all the days of her life …."

We love our lives and the time we share.

I read somewhere a few words that really resonated with me. My version of those words of truth are as follows:

"A man with dreams needs a woman with vision. Her perspective, faith, and support will change his reality. If she doesn't challenge him, she may not be good for him. Men who want to be great expect their partner to push them, pray with them, and invest in them ... to help make them better!"

One of the greatest things in my life is our family! We have a big blended family with lots of kids, grandkids (and more on the way), and even a great-grandchild!

Dreams are everything! I am now financially frugal (I've even been caught by my friends shopping in a thrift store!) and am always open to ways to save money, even though my focus is on making more money ... but when it comes to lifetime memories, there is no expense spared! Memories are what you leave behind one day when you go to a greater life! I want to leave grand memories for my loved ones, not bad ones! So, I try to build fantastic memories!

Sometimes life is about risking everything for a dream that nobody can see except you!

Lucille Ball said, "I'd rather regret the things I've done than regret the things I haven't done!"

So be good to everyone! The Golden Rule says, do unto others as you would have them do unto you! And fall in love with your life!

The happier you are, the more beautiful you become. You can become anything in life you want, so be fearless in the pursuit of what sets your soul on fire!

And remember, no matter who is President, Jesus will always be King!

The life lesson I learned:

If there are different financial values between two people, especially spouses, there are automatic problems in the relationship.

FINANCIAL LESSON:

The best tip I can personally give you for your financial security blanket is a special program that makes me feel totally secure. To get this information, simply text the word PROSPER (in capital letters) to 512-948-3594. This one program could help you develop so much confidence in your financial future!

...

NOTES TO SELF:

ABOUT THE AUTHOR

Larry Smith is an American business success story. He is a highly decorated, two-tour, Vietnam Veteran. He received four Army Commendation (ARCOM) medals, the Bronze Star, and his unit received two Presidential Citations and the Vietnam Cross of Gallantry.

Larry spent 20 years in corporate America. He started at an entry-level sales position with the Pillsbury Company and progressed to District Manager. After 10 years there, he joined a colleague to head up a company in Dallas, Texas. As Director of Sales, he had more than 100 people working with him in launching popular brands like Corona Beer, Pacifico Beer, Bartles and Jaymes Wine Coolers, and more.

He then stepped into the role of President of the US division of a company based in Brisbane, Australia. The company had 32 different divisions worldwide, but it went out of business in 1995, leaving Larry unemployed at age 44.

Larry started a part-time, home-based business in 1996. It quickly turned very profitable earning him more than twice his corporate income in his second year as a business owner.

Today, Larry enjoys a multiple six-figure annual passive income from this business. He has been featured in books, magazines, radio talk shows, and TV for his financial success.

He is the Treasurer on the Board of Directors for Work Play Love, a 501c3 charity organization, dedicated to helping children in Guatemala and Mexico (WorkPlayLove.org).

Larry's genuine hope is that you will take him up on his dare to get rich. For more information on private appointments, coaching sessions, or to book speaking engagements, please go to LoveAndMoneyHacks.com

LoveAndMoneyHacks.com

Powered by Success Strategies, INC